Write your name:

Whenever Snake is scared, he makes himself into an ‹s› shape and hisses, *sssss*.

S s

S
S
s
S
S
S

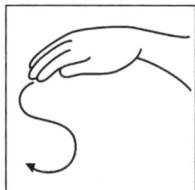

Action: Weave your hand in an ‹s› shape like a snake and say *sssss*.

Trace over the dotted lines, keeping inside the snakes.

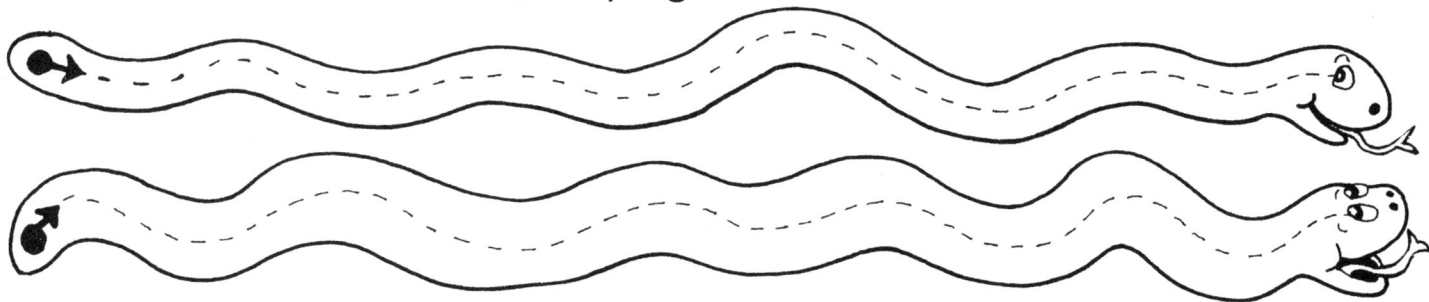

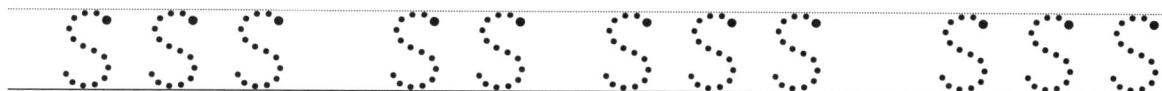

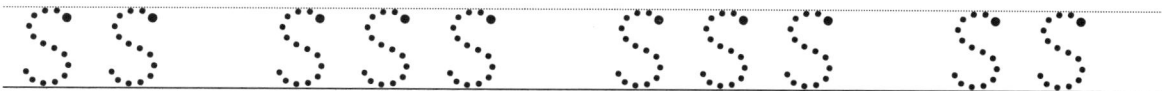

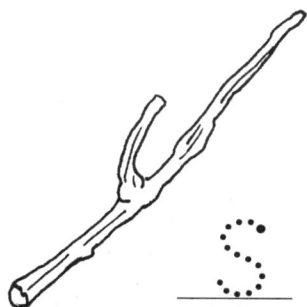

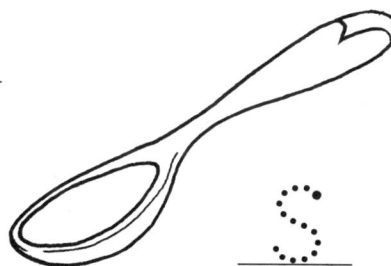

S

SSS SS SSS SSS

SS SSS SS SSS SS

S

S

S

S

S

A a

The ants have found a picnic. Some of the ants crawl up the girl's arm. She looks down and says *a, a, a, a, ants!*

Action: Wiggle your fingers up your arm as if ants are crawling on you, and say *a, a, a, a!*

Follow the ants to reach the anthill.

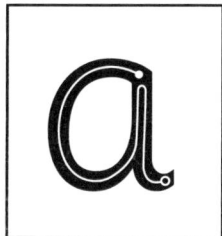

a

a a a a a a a a a

a a a a a a a a

a

a

a

a

T t

Two children are playing tennis. They hit the ball to each other, *t, t, t, t.*

Action: Turn your head from side to side as if you are watching tennis, and say *t, t, t, t.*

Follow the bouncing ball.

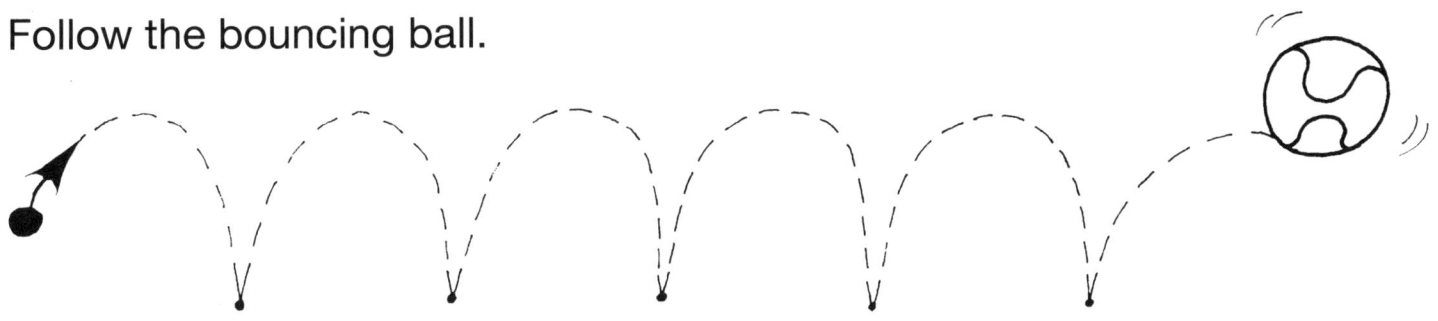

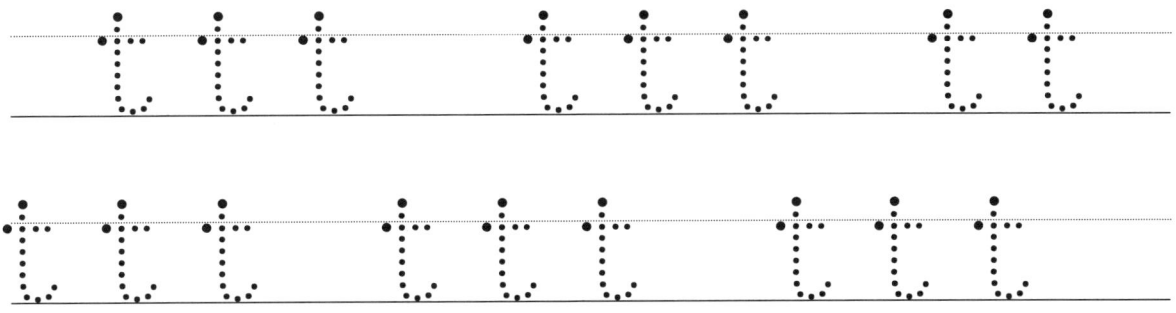

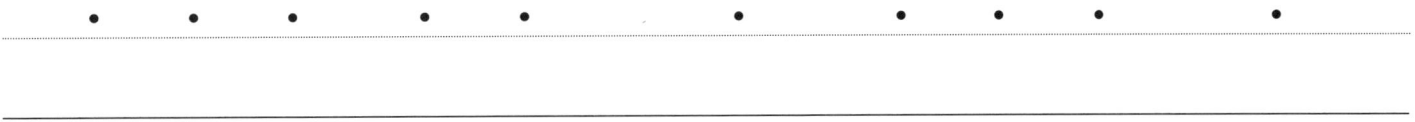

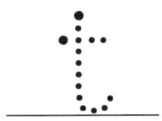

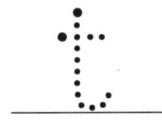

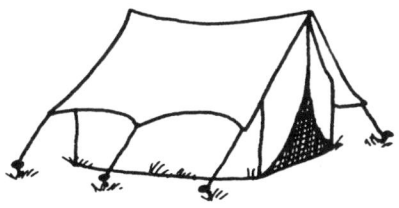

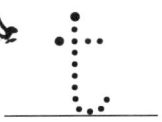

t

t t t   t t t   t t
t t t   t t t   t t t

I i

Inky Mouse got her name because she was covered in ink when she escaped from her cage.

Action: Wiggle your fingers at the end of your nose as if you are a mouse stroking its whiskers, and squeak *i, i, i, i.*

Follow the trail to find Inky.

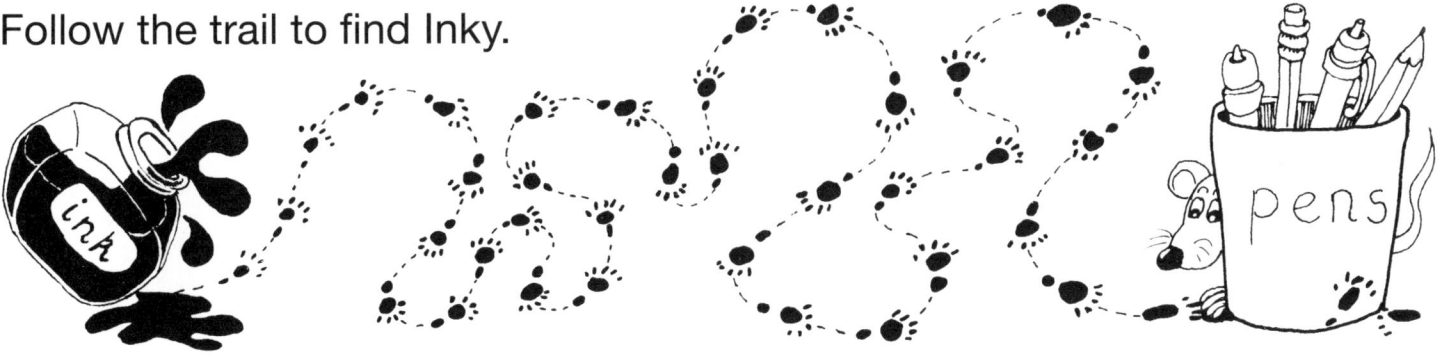

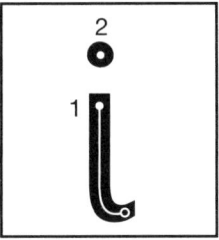

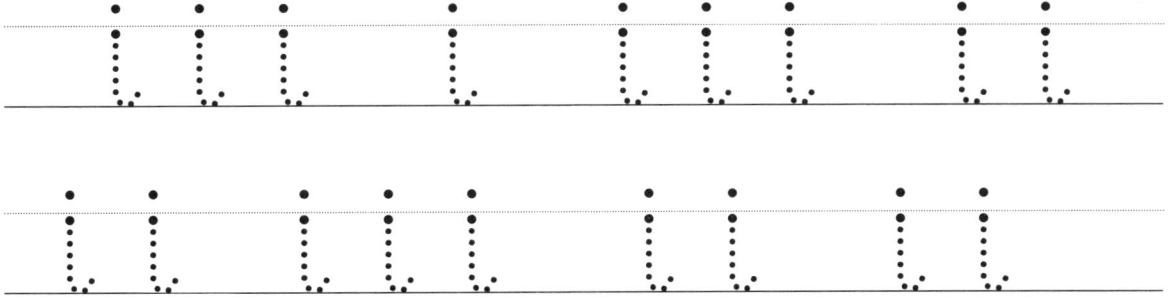

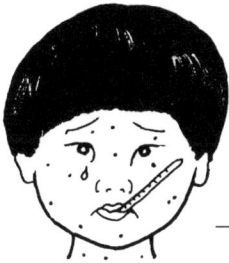

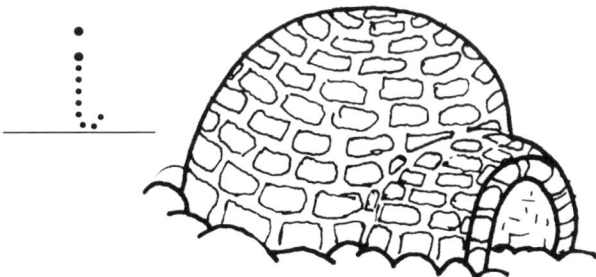

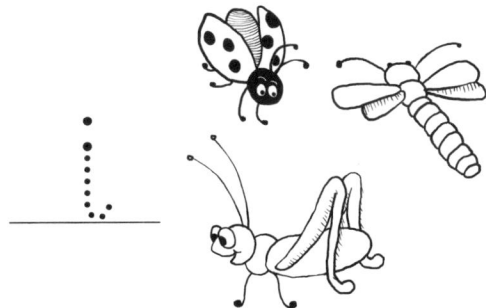

It is Bee's birthday. Inky has made a pink party cake with 3 candles to puff out, *p, p, p.*

P p

Action: Hold up your finger as if it is a candle and pretend to puff it out, saying *p, p, p, p.*

10

Show the penguin the way to the igloo.

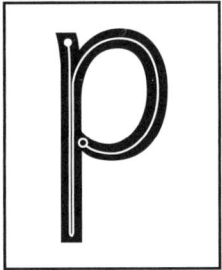

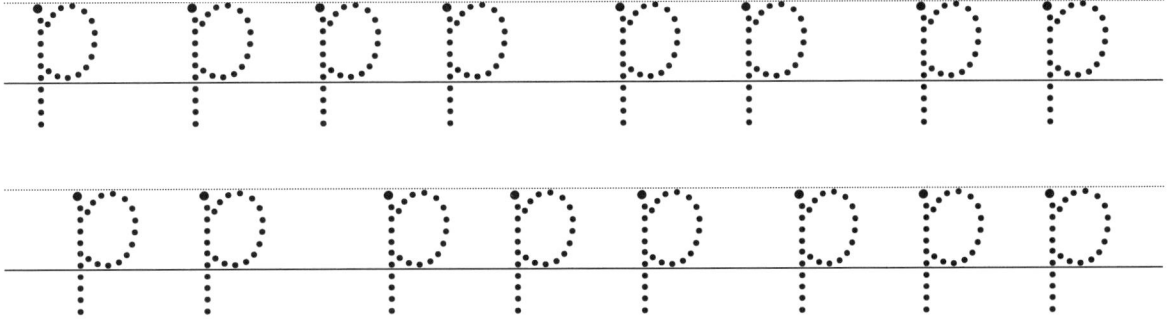

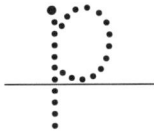

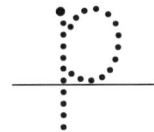

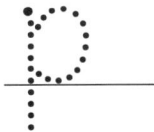

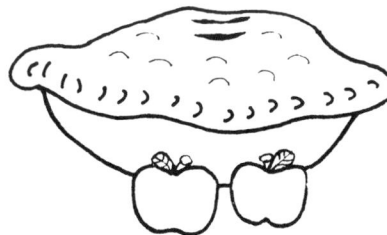

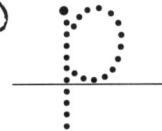

p p p p p p p p p p

p p p p p p p p p p

N n

Inky is woken up by a nasty noise. There is a model plane flying about, going *nnnnnn*.

Action: Pretend to be a plane with your arms out like wings, and say *nnnnnn*.

Help the robin to his nest.

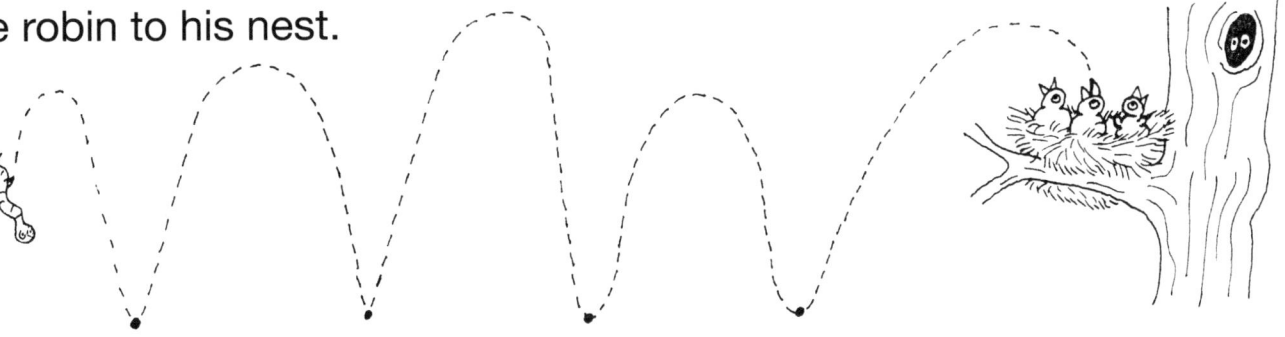

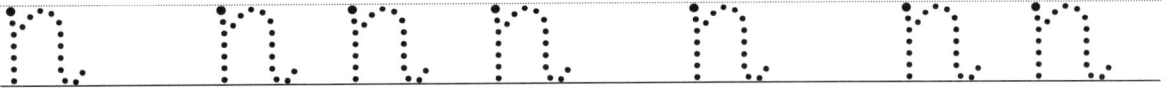

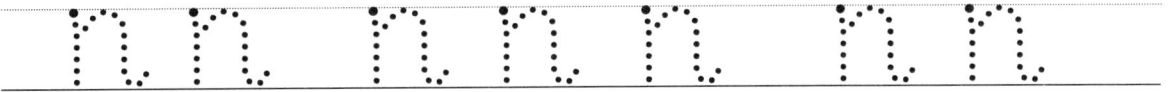

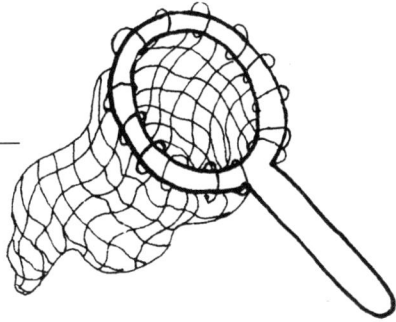

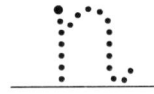

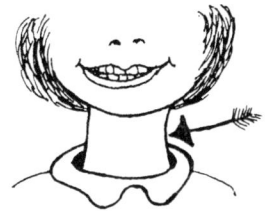

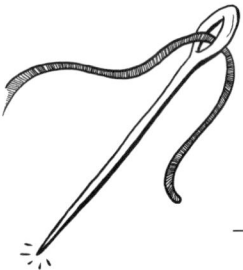

n

n n n n n n n

n n n n n n n

13

Trace over the dotted lines to make each pair of snakes the same.

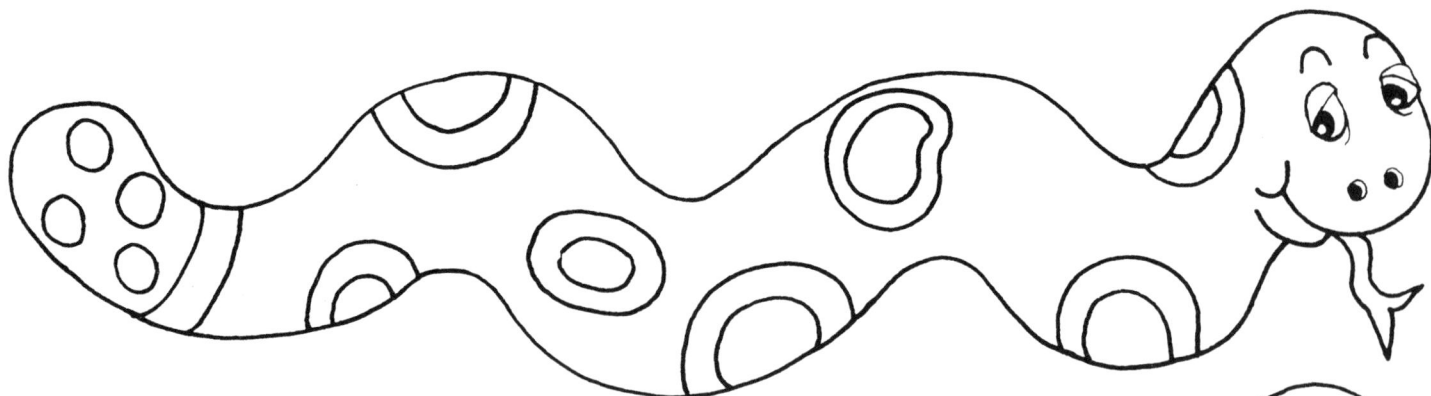

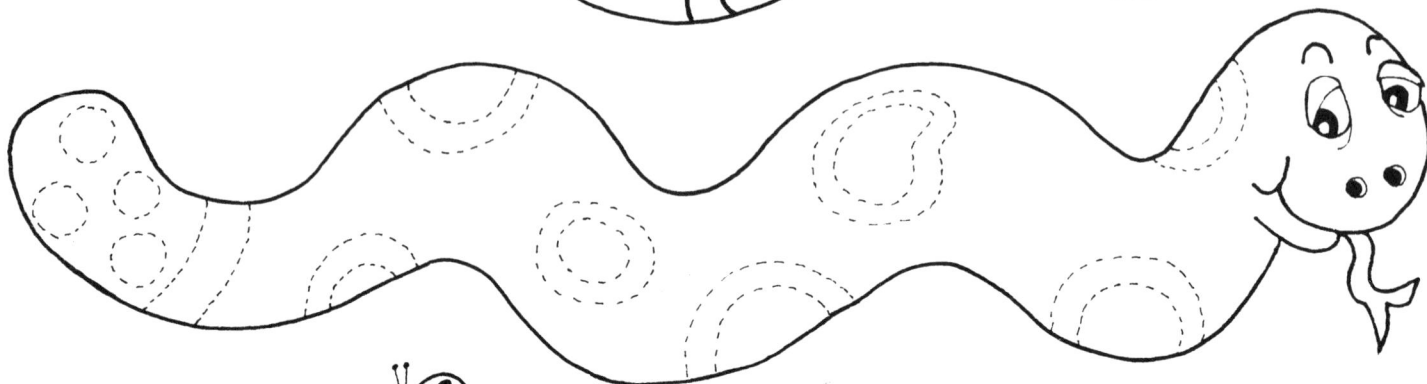

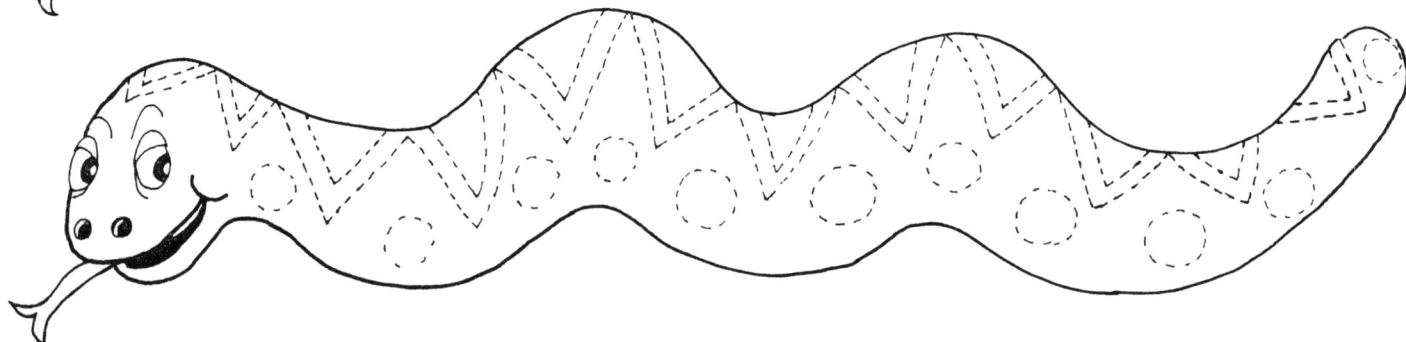

Join each picture to the letter for the sound it begins with.

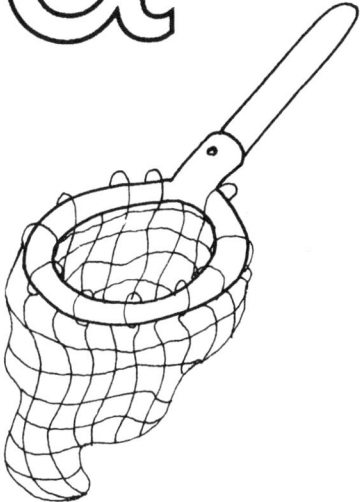

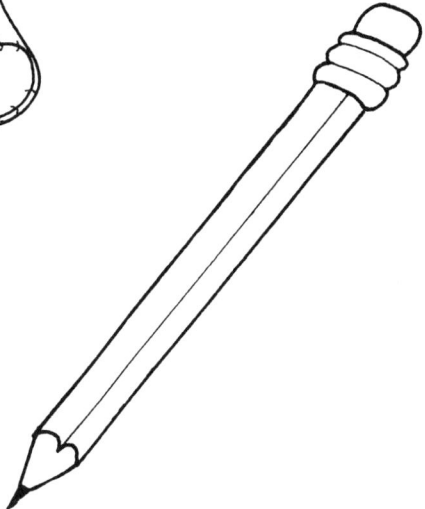

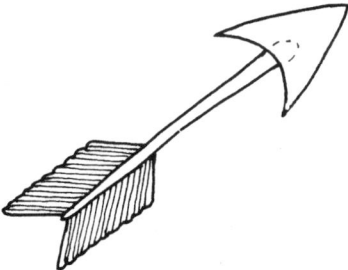

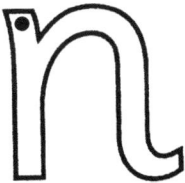

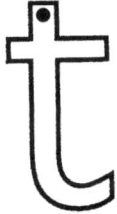

a

i

p

s

n

t

Follow the trails.

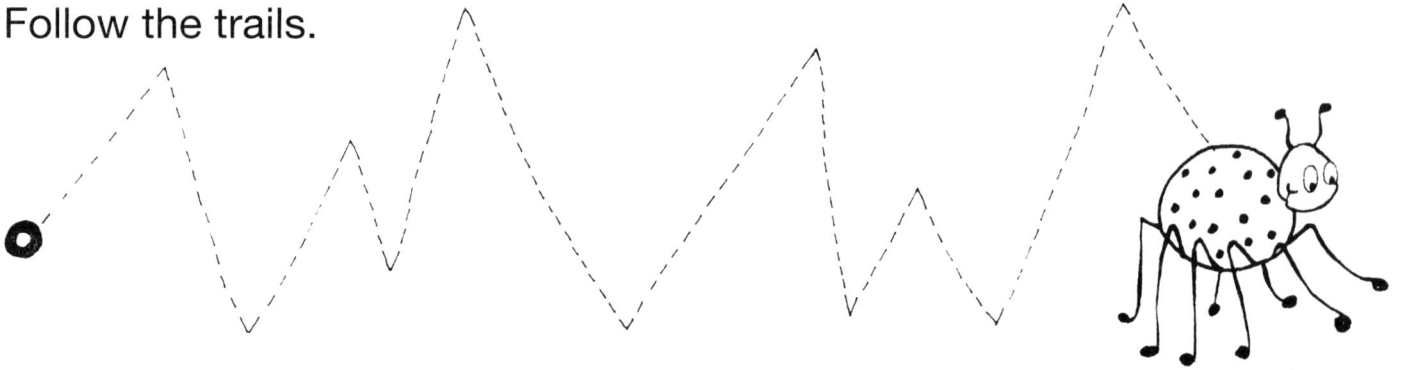

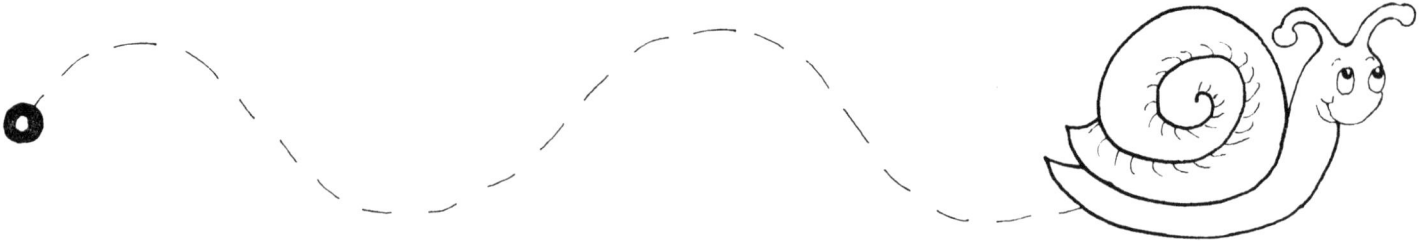

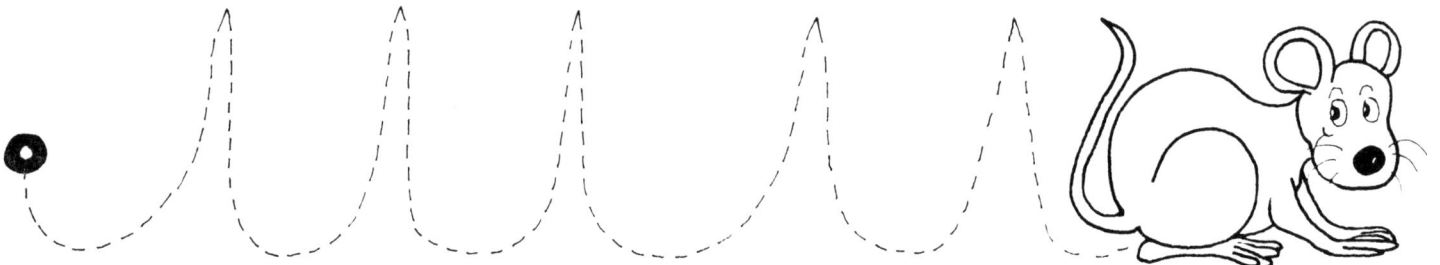

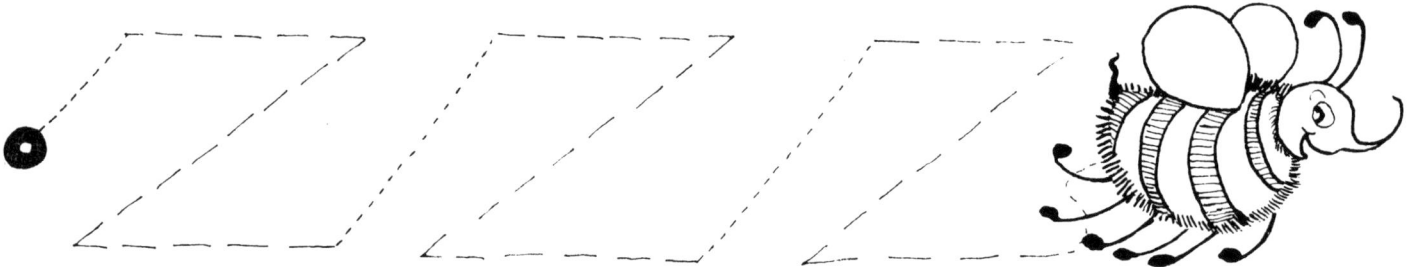

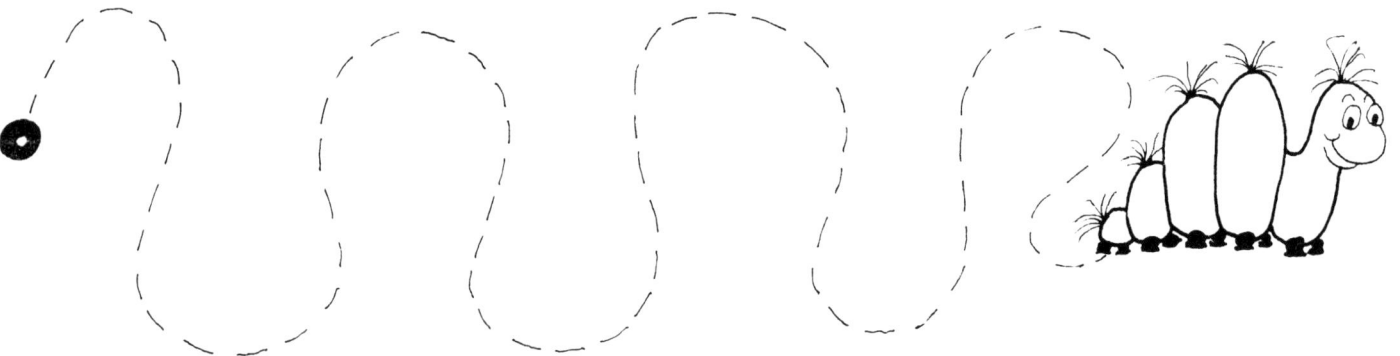

Write the letter for the first sound in each word.

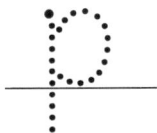

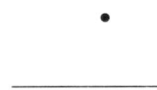

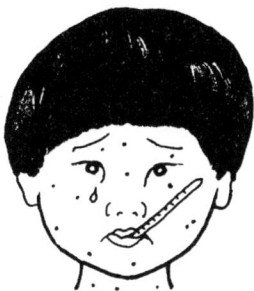

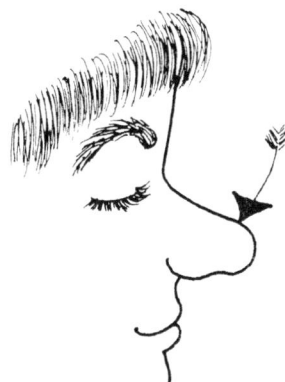

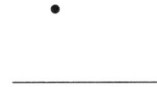

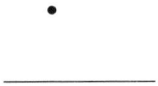

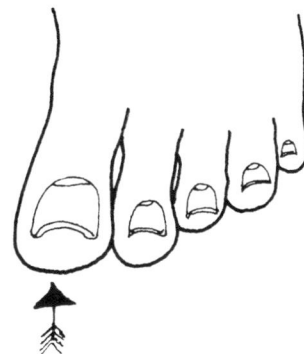

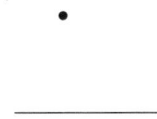

p

a

.

.

.

.

.

.

.

.

Put the spots on the snakes.

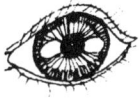 Spy things beginning with the same sound.

a

t

s

p

n

i

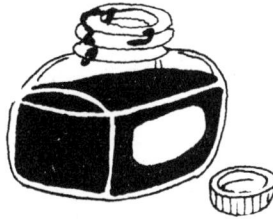

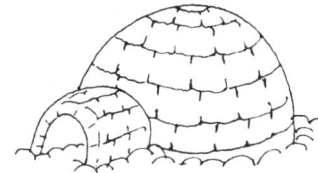

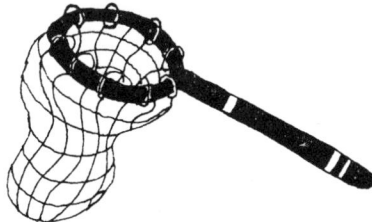

Some more writing practice. Can you think of something that begins with each sound and draw it?

s   s   .   .   .   .   .

a   a   .   .   .   .   .

t   t   .   .   .   .   .

i   i   .   .   .   .   .

p   p   .   .   .   .   .

n   n   .   .   .   .   .

Look at each picture and the letter written next to it. Can you hear the sound for that letter at the beginning of the word?

s ✓

i x

n ☐

a ☐

p ☐

t ☐

Write the words, then read them. To do this, say the sound for each letter in turn and listen for the word.

at

it

in

sat

pin

pit

tin

pat

sit

The sounds must be said quickly to hear the word. It is easier if the first sound is slightly louder: /s-a-t/.

Numbers need correct formation, just as letters do.

1 Snake

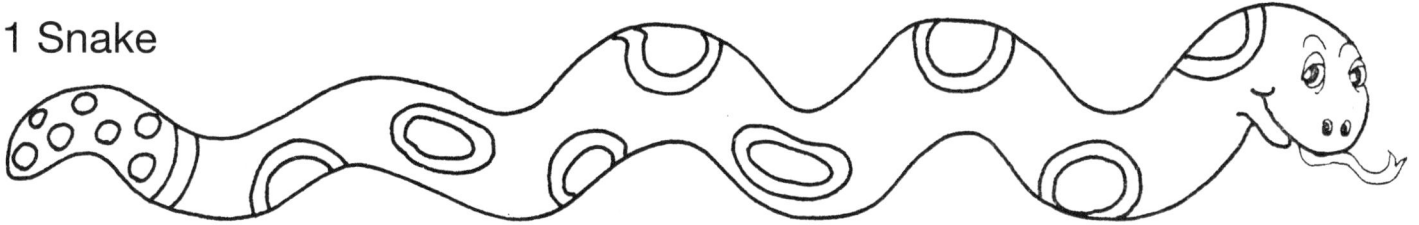

Trace over the dotted lines to write the number 1.

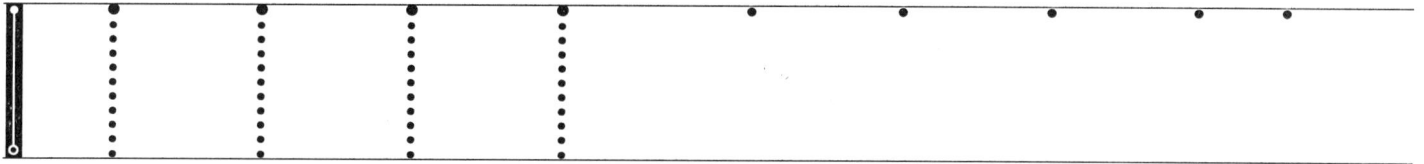

Where is Snake?

Activity

Make your own sound book

Curly Snake

On a piece of paper, draw a curled-up snake. Paint or decorate him, then cut around and around to make him uncurl. Then you can hang him up.

Inky pictures

Make some inky pictures. Put some ink or paint on one half of a piece of paper. Fold it in half and press down.

Open up the paper and look at the ink. What does it look like? Can you make it into a picture?